D0623976

WEB PAGE Design

Clive Gifford

Crabtree Publishing Company
www.crabtreebooks.com

Crabtree Publishing Company
www.crabtreebooks.com
1-800-387-7650

Published in Canada
Crabtree Publishing
616 Welland Ave.
St. Catharines, ON
L2M 5V6

Published in the United States
Crabtree Publishing
PMB 59051, 350 Fifth Ave.
59th Floor,
New York, NY

Published in 2018 by CRABTREE PUBLISHING COMPANY.

First published in 2017 by Wayland
(A division of Hachette Children's Books)

Author: Clive Gifford
Project editor: Sonya Newland
Designer: Rocket Design Ltd
Editors: Sonya Newland, Kathy Middleton
Proofreader: Petrice Custance
Prepress technician: Ken Wright
Print and production coordinator: Margaret Amy Salter

Consultant: Lee Martin, B. Ed, E-Learning Specialist

Printed in the USA / 072017 / CG20170524

Photographs:
All images courtesy of Shutterstock except:
Big Blu Books: p.12l; iStock: 26r (golibo);
Wikimedia: p.22b (Heinrich-Böll-Stiftung).

While every attempt has been made to clear copyright, should there be any inadvertent omission this will be rectified in future editions.

Disclaimer: The website addresses (URLs) included in this book were valid at the time of going to press. However, because of the nature of the Internet, it is possible that some addresses may have changed, or sites may have changed or closed down since publication. While the author and publisher regret any inconvenience this may cause the readers, no responsibility for any such changes can be accepted by either the author or the publisher.

Note to reader: Words highlighted in bold appear in the Glossary on page 30.
Answers to activities are on page 31.

Library and Archives Canada Cataloguing in Publication

Gifford, Clive, author
Web page design / Clive Gifford.

(Get connected to digital literacy)
Includes index.
Issued in print and electronic formats.
ISBN 978-0-7787-3631-8 (hardcover).--
ISBN 978-0-7787-3635-6 (softcover).--
ISBN 978-1-4271-1960-5 (HTML)

1. Web sites--Design--Juvenile literature. 2. Computer programming--Juvenile literature. 3. World Wide Web--Juvenile literature. 4. Internet--Juvenile literature. I. Title.

TK5105.888.G542 2017 j006.7 C2017-903185-6
C2017-903186-4

Library of Congress Cataloging-in-Publication Data

CIP available at the Library of Congress

Contents

From its humble start, running on a single computer, the **World Wide Web** (better known by the letters www) has become the world's biggest source of information and entertainment. Every day, hundreds of millions of people turn to the Web to look at pages of images, text, and videos.

What is the Web?

Some people think that the **Internet** and the World Wide Web are the same thing. They are not.

- The Internet is the name given to the giant system of computer networks that spans the world. It connects millions of computers, allowing them to send digital **data** such as emails or files to one another.
- The World Wide Web is a collection of information that can be accessed using the Internet. The Web consists of millions of websites containing documents, links, and files. These can be viewed by almost any device that can access the Internet.

People use smartphones, tablets, and **smart** TVs, as well as computers, to access the Internet.

Web explosion

When the World Wide Web was established, home computers were still in their early development, so not many people had access to the Internet. In 1993, there were just 130 websites. As home computers became more popular, so did the Web. By 2000, there were 17 million websites.

Site types

Today, there are over one billion websites around the world! Some are simple, single-page ads or personal pages created by individuals. Others are built by companies or governments. Some websites are vast, containing thousands of different pages. By 2017, the English-language edition of the encyclopedia website Wikipedia contained over 5.3 million pages.

COMPUTER Hero!

British computer scientist Tim Berners-Lee worked at a major science research center in Switzerland called CERN. He was interested in finding new ways for scientists to share their information. With the help of colleagues, Berners-Lee invented the **HTML** coding language (see page 12) for creating **web pages.** He developed the rules, known as **HTTP,** to transmit the web pages over the Internet. He also created the first web page and **web server.** Berners-Lee launched the Internet to the world on Christmas day in 1990.

Tim Berners-Lee

TRUE STORY

What's in a Name? The World Wide Web was nearly called the Information Mesh, The Project, or the Mine of Information. Berners-Lee and his colleagues considered all these names before opting for World Wide Web.

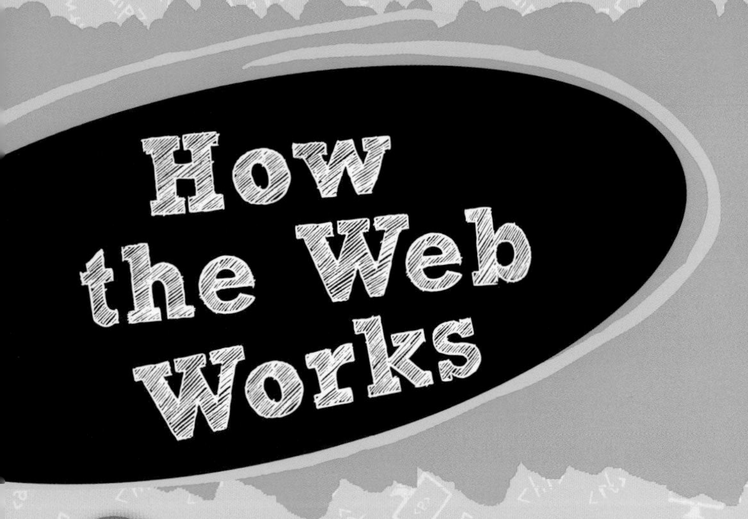

How the Web Works

When you access the World Wide Web through a computer, smartphone, or tablet, your simple request to see a web page involves a number of computers and programs all working together.

Web servers

Web servers are powerful computers that store all the files and data, or information, needed to display a website. Computers or digital devices such as smartphones and tablets that communicate with the web server are known as **clients**.

Keeping track

Web servers keep track of which page to send to a client by using the web page's **URL**. Short for Uniform Resource Locator, this is the address of a web page on the World Wide Web. All web pages, and other files on the Web, such as music or video files, have their own unique URL.

A user, whose computer is the client, types the address of the web page they want to see.

The request travels over the Internet to the web server that holds that web page. The server searches through its storage for the right files.

The server sends the web page over the Internet back to the client. The computer displays the page on its screen.

Understanding URLs

A URL often looks like this:

http://www.clivelive.com/aboutme.html

http
This stands for the protocol. Protocol is a series of rules and codes that help one computer talk to another.

www
This tells the server that the file's location can be found on the World Wide Web.

clivelive.com
In this example, this is the name of the website. It is also called its **domain name**.

aboutme.html
This is the name of the file that is being requested. In this example, it is a web page, but it could be an image or music file.

Browsing around

When the web page that has been requested arrives, it is displayed on the client's computer or device by a program called a **web browser** (or just browser). Popular browsers include Mozilla Firefox, Google Chrome, Safari, Internet Explorer, and Opera. They all tend to have the same main buttons and features.

Address bar
This is where you type in URLs or topics to search for.

Back and **Forward**
These buttons allow you to leave the web page you are on and come back to it again.

Refresh
This button reloads the web page you are on to see if it has been updated. Sometimes it also helps fix a page that will not load.

Home
This button will take you back to the home page of the browser you are using.

To create websites, you need a web browser, an Internet connection, a website domain name, a web host, and programs to write and send web pages.

Domain names

A website needs its own unique address so that people can search for it. The domain name is the most unique part of the URL address. The code to the right of the period, or dot, is called the top level domain. In the example clivelive.com, "com" is the top level domain and stands for commercial business. It tells you something about the website's purpose. Another example is "edu" which means it is related to education. It could also be a country code, such as "us" for United States. The code to the left of the dot is called the mid level domain. It is a name specific to the owner, for example, "clivelive."

DOT WHAT?

An official organization determines top level domain names. Recent additions include "farm," "social," and even "ninja"!

STRETCH YOURSELF

Name Your Site

Come up with your perfect website name. Try to keep the name short and think up alternatives in case it is already taken. For example, if Hamsters.com is already taken, why not try Myhamsters.com or something similar? Type the following address into your web browser:

https://who.is/

You can put your website name in the box at the top and see if it is available. If it is already taken, you can see who registered the name and on what date.

Web hosting

A website needs to be stored on a web server so that it can be accessed over the Internet. This service is provided by a company called a web host. There are hundreds of web-hosting companies, and many offer packages that include the domain name and tools that make it easier to build websites.

TRUE STORY

Ka-ching Dot Com!

Some people make money just by buying and selling domain names. In 2000, American computer consultant Marcelo Siero sold a domain name he got for free in 1994. The name loans.com sold for a cool $3 million US!

Uploading

A web page is created on a designer's computer or tablet. It is saved on that device and then **uploaded** to a web server. Most pages are served using a set of rules called File Transfer Protocol (**FTP**).

Website writer

Websites are written in a coding language called HTML, using a program to edit text such as Notepad or TextEdit. Some people use more complex programs, such as Sublime Text or Google Web Designer, to design their web pages. These programs let you drag and drop bits of an existing web page onto part of the screen and see the code that produced it.

A web designer sketches out the overall look of a web page on a see-through screen. He is mapping out where images and text will appear before the web page is coded.

A Selection of Sites

Before you get started building or even planning your own website, it is worth looking at other sites to check out different designs, types, and features.

Sites that share

Members on social media websites, such as Facebook, Twitter, and Instagram, become part of communities that allow users to share photos, personal updates, and other information. Other sharing websites, such as Instructables.com, give access to human-made projects and expert advice.

News and sports

Back in 1995, British schoolboy Tom Hadfield was just 12 years old when he built one of the first websites to feature sports scores. Five years later, he sold his SoccerNet website to the sports channel ESPN. Today, the Web has become the first source people go to for news, sports, and information.

Online shopping

The Web also brought us a whole new way to shop. Many websites are created for online business called e-commerce. Buying and selling goods and services over the Internet resulted in sales of over $1.9 trillion US in 2016. That's about $6,000 US for every one of the nearly 320 million people who live in the United States!

Website warnings

There are so many websites on the Web, the amount of choice can be confusing. To make matters more difficult, not all websites are truthful, up to date, or accurate. Websites produced by major libraries, museums, and respected organizations, such as PBS or National Geographic, are generally reliable sources to get information from.

TRUE STORY

Mammoth Sales

Some strange things have been sold on the auction website eBay. The first ever item was a broken laser pointer that sold for $14.83 US in 1995. In 1994, the remains of a 50,000-year-old woolly mammoth weighing about 550,000 pounds (250,000 kg) was sold on eBay for 61,000 British pounds(back then, about $12,000 US)!

Types of Websites

There are many different types of websites, with different purposes:

- Business websites help people research companies and find the one with the best offer for what they are looking for.
- Information websites, such as Wikipedia or Encyclopedia Britannica, serve as sources of general information on different topics.
- Directory websites are collections of website addresses grouped within subject categories to help people find specific information.
- Forums are websites that allow people to communicate with one another, ask questions about certain subjects, and share information.

STRETCH YOURSELF

Homework Helpers

Pick a science topic you're interested in, such as rockets, computer viruses, or the human eye, and see what useful information you can find at the reliable educational websites below. Write down how the websites differ in design and the ways they display information.

- kids.britannica.com
- www.explainthatstuff.com
- www.sciencenewsforstudents.org

Hypertext Markup Language (HTML) is the language used to develop web pages. HTML's elements and **tags** tell the web browser how to display the page, but these elements cannot be seen by visitors on the final page.

See the source

To see the HTML code behind a web page, you can right click on a mouse while viewing a web page, then select "view source" or "source" from the drop-down menu at the top. On PCs, you can do it by holding down the "CTRL" and "U" keys on your keyboard.

Play tag

HTML is built with tags. These are brackets that look like these: < >. Code, or lines of text that instruct the browser, is contained inside the brackets. For example, the code <hr> is an instruction that means draw a horizontal line.

Most instructions are made up of a pair of tags. The instruction begins with a start, or opening, tag and is completed by an end, or closing, tag. You can recognize an end tag because, unlike an opening tag, it has a forward slash (/) inside the bracket.

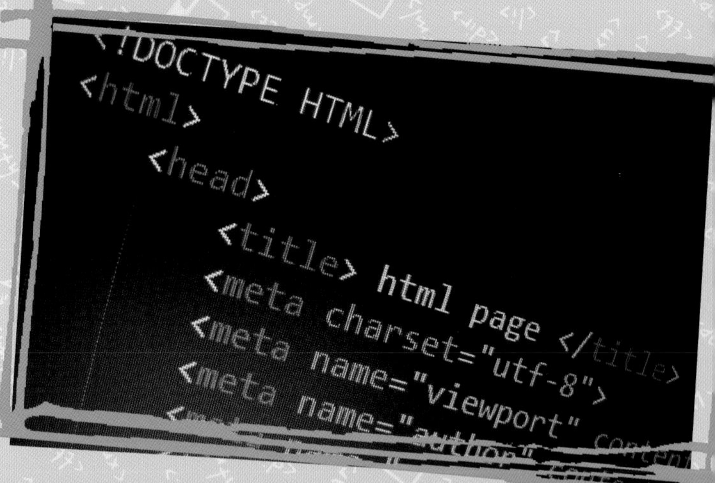

Text tags

HTML tags act on the text of a web page, changing it in some way. Some of the most common tags are shown below, along with what they do.

<u>This text is underlined</u>	This text is underlined
<strong>This text is in bold</strong>	**This text is in bold**
<em>This text is emphasized and in italics</em>	*This text is emphasized and in italics*
<center>This text is centered</center>	This text is centered

Heading master

Tags let you create larger text headings for parts of your page. There are six levels of headings available, from the largest <h1>, down to the smallest <h6>. Look at the box to the right to see how the codes below affect the type.

```
<h1>H1 Biggest Heading</h1>
<h2>H2 Heading</h2>
<h3>H3 Heading</h3>
<h4>H4 Heading</h4>
<h5>H5 Headings getting smaller</h5>
<h6>And H6, the smallest</h6>
```

H1 Biggest Heading
H2 Heading
H3 Heading
H4 Heading
H5 Headings getting smaller
And H6, the smallest

REMEMBER!
In HTML code, all quotation marks should be straight (") not curly (“ or ”).

Tag-tastic

You can use more than one tag on a piece of text. For example, if you want the words "My Story" to be a heading and also be emphasized in italics, write the HTML this way:

```
<h1><em>My Story</em></h1>
```

COLOR CODED

Text on an HTML page can also have its color changed from black by using the style tag. For example:

```
<p style= "color:red;">Red is the color</p>
```

will result in: Red is the color

The latest version of HTML includes 140 standard colors. See all the named colors by typing the following into your browser:

www.w3schools.com/colors/colors_names.asp

For a page to be displayed correctly by a browser, the HTML page has to follow a particular structure. HTML pages can be written in a simple text-editor program by opening a new file, typing in the code, and then saving the file.

```
<!DOCTYPE html PUBLIC "-//W3C
<html xmlns="http://www.w3.or
  <head>
    <meta http-equiv="Content-
    <meta http-equiv="Content-
    <meta http-equiv="Content-
    <title>Document Title</ti
    <link rev="made" href="mai
    <link rev="start" href="./
    <style type="text/css" me
```

At the start

All web pages start with <!DOCTYPE html>. This lets the browser know that it is receiving an HTML document. It is followed by the tag <html>. This signals the start of the web page. At the very bottom will be the tag </html>, which ends the page.

Header and body

The title of the web page goes between the two header tags <head> and </head>. The parts of an HTML document that actually appear on the web page are all the pictures, text, and tables found between the tags <body> and </body>.

Paragraph tag

Paragraphs are defined in HTML with the opening tag <p> and the closing tag </p>. Browsers automatically put a bit of space between paragraphs, so it is a good way to divide up text on a web page.

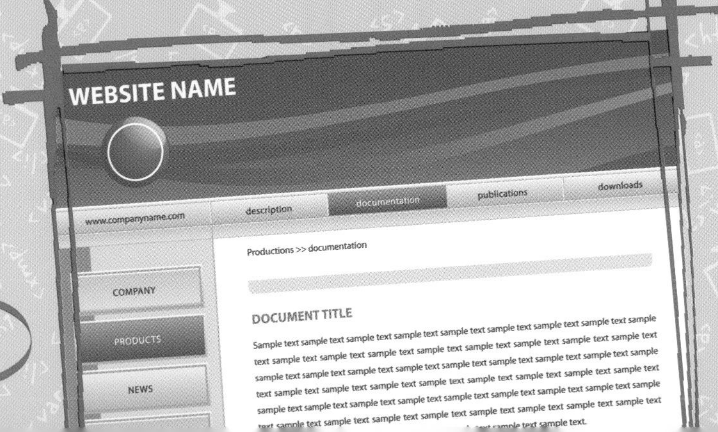

STRETCH YOURSELF

Make Your First Page

Follow these steps to create your own first web page. Get someone to help you with any stages you are not sure about.

1. Make a new folder on your computer called "My Web Pages."
2. Open a text-editor program such as Notepad or TextEdit. Type in the web page html code in the panel that appears to the right.
3. Change the heading and the text between the tags <p> and </p> to whatever you want them to say.
4. Save the page in your new folder and give it a name ending in .html.
5. Double click quickly on your new file. A web browser program should open and display your page as it would appear on a website.

A Simple Page

```
<!DOCTYPE html>
<html>
<head>
<title>My First Web Page</title>
</head>
<body>
<h1>The heading for the page</h1>
<p>This is where all my words will go in the first paragraph</p>
<hr>
<h3>Smaller heading</h3>
<p>This is where the words will go for the second paragraph.</p>
</body>
</html>
```

TAG AFTER TAG

There are a lot of HTML tags. You can view a complete list by typing the following address into your web browser:

www.htmldog.com/references/html/tags/

Click on any tag and a page appears that describes what the tag is used for along with a real example in HTML code.

Adding Images

There are still a handful of websites made up only of text. Today, most sites are packed with pictures to add interest and excitement to a web page. You can store all your website images in an "Images" folder on your computer.

Free to use

If you want to use images from a website, you usually have to ask their permission to do so. However, some websites offer free images, including:

https://search.creativecommons.org/

www.freeimages.co.uk/galleries.htm

You can take your own photos to add to your website, or create original artwork and then scan it.

Image tag

A single tag is all that's required to add an image in HTML. It does not need a closing tag. An image tag looks like this:

```
<img src= "/webpix/picture.jpg" >
```

img
An HTML tag that tells the browser that an image will go here.

src
Stands for source. It tells the browser where to go to gather the image that is to be displayed.

webpix
Identifies the folder the image is found in.

picture.jpg
The name of the image file. You can name the file whatever you want. The folder and image names should always be enclosed together in quotation marks.

Bigger or smaller?

Your image file might be bigger than the size you want to show it on the web page. You can resize it using an **app** (see below) or you can change its height and width in the HTML code.

The image's height and width are given in number of **pixels**. These are dots that combine to make an image on the screen. Increasing the number of pixels gives you a bigger image. Decreasing the number makes it smaller. In HTML code, the numbers should always be enclosed in quotation marks.

This image is 180 pixels wide and 120 pixels high. It is represented in code by this:

<img src="/images/petdog.jpg" width="180" height="120">

This image is half the height and width of the original. The tag changes to:

<img src="/images/petdog.jpg" width="90" height="60">

This image has been stretched so that it is wider than the original but the same height.

<img src="/images/petdog.jpg" width="300" height="120">

STRETCH YOURSELF

Apps for Resizing

There are apps online that allow you to resize your photos. Try one out by typing the following address into your browser:

http://webresizer.com/resizer/

Try turning your picture black and white using the monochrome button. Or add a colored border to your image.

1. Press the "Choose file" button. Select an image on your computer or device to resize, then press the "Upload image" button.
2. You will see two pictures. Below them is a set of boxes. Enter a different number of pixels in the "New size" box.
3. Select "Apply changes," and the resized image will appear on the page in the box to the left. Click on the "Download this image" button to bring the resized image to your computer.

To produce a website, you need to think about what content it will contain, and how it will be organized into different web pages with links to each other.

Hyperlinks

To link different parts of a website together, web pages use **hyperlinks**. A hyperlink is text or images that have been coded to take users from one place to another when clicked on. Text with a hyperlink is usually underlined or in a different color. When the text or an image with a hyperlink is clicked on, the link tells the browser to jump to another page or element on the World Wide Web.

WHAT SHOULD I DO NOW?

Click the link below for other titles.

See Other Great Books.

This is a list of highly recommended books to read.

In 1960, American Ted Nelson began Project Xanadu. His goal was to build the first easy-to-use computer network. He invented hyperlinks, which allowed information to be easily accessed. His work influenced other information technology pioneers, such as Douglas Engelbart, who invented the computer mouse, and Tim Berners-Lee, who came up with the World Wide Web.

Local or external

A hyperlink can instruct the browser to head to another page on the same website. This is called a local link. A link can also jump to a different website. This is called an external link.

The website address is where the browser will go. It is not displayed on the web page.

```
<a href="https://www.crabtreebooks.com/"> Meet
Author Bobbie Kalman</a>
```

This text is displayed as a hyperlink.

This tag ends the hyperlink.

Not just text

Hyperlinks are used for more than just text. An image can also be turned into a hyperlink.

This is the address of a gallery web page of cat images.

This tag adds a cat image. It acts as a hyperlink which can be clicked on to go to the gallery.

```
<a href="websiteaddress/
catpix"> <img src="tabbycat.jpg"> </a>
```

Sketch a Site Map

Using pens and paper, plan out the perfect site map. Draw a large rectangle for each web page and write in what it will contain. Draw lines to show how the pages will link to each other. Think about the following questions:

- How do you want people to use your website?
- Which pages do you think they will visit most?
- What sort of menu will you have and what will its buttons say?
- Where will you include hyperlinks?

Menu matters

A website's menu is the list of sections the site is divided into. The menu section, or bar, runs across the top of the page or down one side. Hyperlinks are used to create menu items. Each button is a word or image with a hyperlink in the HTML code. Clicking on one gives users quick access to a section.

To make a great web page, you need a good eye, interesting content, and HTML knowledge. Try to make your pages easy for users to read, view, and **navigate**.

Writing for the Web

Writing text for websites is different than writing an essay. Studies show that you have only seconds to grab a viewer's attention. People tend to glance at a web page and read only parts of it. Make sure the most important part of your message is clearly stated near the top of the web page.

Paragraphs should be short and to the point. If you refer to another page on the site, create a hyperlink to it instead of repeating the text. Split the text up into sections with interesting headings. This is called chunking. It will help keep your visitors reading.

Making Lists

Putting text in short, neat lists can keep your web page looking clean and uncluttered. You can number each item, which is called ordered list by using the tag <ol>. Unordered lists use the tag <ul>. This creates a list using bullet points.

Code for an unordered list (note: <li> = list item):

```
<strong>My favorite things</strong><ul>
<li>My game console</li>
<li>My best friend, Steve</li>
<li>My mountain bike</li>
<li>Pizza for dinner!</li></ul>
```

The list will look like this:

My favorite things

- My game console
- My best friend, Steve
- My mountain bike
- Pizza for dinner!

Dividing It Up

The tag <div> can also be useful in the design of your web page. It can be used to split up sections of a web page so that different styles apply to sections. For example, you can give a section of the page a pink background by adding the following HTML code:

```
<div style="background-color: pink">
<h2>Pink Part of Page heading</h2>
<p>Here is a paragraph placed on a
pink background</p>
<p>And here is another<p>
</div>
<p>This paragraph is not part of the pink section.</p>
```

TRUE STORY

Chair Man! You're never too young to become a successful website designer. American Sean Kelnick was just 14 years old when he built the BizChair. com website. Six years later, it was selling $38 million US in office chairs every year!

WEB PAGE CHECKLIST

Make a habit of checking all these things before you complete a page:

- ☐ Do all your tags have a closing tag if they need one, i.e. </strong>?
- ☐ Have you put a forward slash before the tag element to close it correctly?
- ☐ Are you saving the web page with the correct name?
- ☐ Are all your images the right size? Are the files stored in the correct folders?
- ☐ If you have changed the location of the page on your website, have you changed the menu hyperlinks, too?

Doing It in Style

To make their design choices apply to all pages on a website, many web designers put all their instructions for how the web pages will look into a single document called a **style sheet**.

Benefits of a style sheet

A style sheet saves the web designer's work. A single style sheet can be shared and used by all the web pages of a website. Without it, code for design instructions and edits would have to be written for every single web page.

What is CSS?

CSS stands for Cascading Style Sheets. It defines what colors, panels, and background images will look like on the web pages. CSS files can be created using a text editor program in the same way as an HTML page. To apply CSS to an entire web page, you just have to add a line of code in the header of a web page, such as:

```
<link rel="stylesheet" type="text/css" href="stylesheetfile.css"/>
```

Håkon Wium Lie

COMPUTER Hero!

Håkon Wium Lie was a young Norwegian computer programmer in the 1990s. While working with Tim Berners-Lee on the early World Wide Web, he developed the idea of CSS. It has since become a standard for web design. Lie is now the Chief Technology Officer of the web browser company Opera Software. He is also a politician in Norway's Pirate Party!

Font fun

Let's look at one example of how CSS can change the look of a web page. A font, or typeface, is a specific design or style of type. Here are some common fonts:

Arial Black

Times New Roman

Verdana

Courier New

The height and size of a font is measured in points or pixels. The bigger the number, the bigger the text.

Arial Black 8 point

Arial Black 12 point

Arial Black 16 point

Using CSS, you can change the font, its color, and its size. In the line of code, each characteristic and its value is separated from the next one by a semi-colon. For example:

Verdana

```
p {font-family:"Verdana"; font-
size: 16pt; color: blue;}
```

Text is in blue in the Verdana font and is 16 points in size.

STRETCH YOURSELF

CSS in Action

For a great lesson on how CSSs work and are used, type the following address into your web browser:

http://bit.ly/2s03BEK

Learn how to add style elements to a web page using a CSS, then take it a step further to put all of your elements in place using CSS layout techniques. What can you create?

REMEMBER!
American spelling is used in CSS. For example, "color" should never have a "u."

Some companies make building a website easier for people who don't know how to code. They offer customers a content management system (**CMS**) which makes building and changing a website easy.

One-stop solutions

There are companies, such as Wix and Weebly, that allow you to create an entire website using a **template** for a web page that already has code in it. For example, you can choose your website's look from different design templates. Then you can add different elements, such as text, photos, and menu buttons, to the web page by dragging and dropping them from a menu. Elements can be changed in size, position, and color before the page is sent to the World Wide Web.

CMS

All the text, images, and other elements that go on your web page are called its content. A CMS is a program, or series of programs, that makes it easier to create new content and add it to website pages without writing new HTML code.

Wordpress

People add many different CMSs to their websites, including Joomla, Squarespace, and Magento. The most popular is Wordpress, which powers over a quarter of all websites that use CMSs. In 2015, one million new articles were published each day on Wordpress sites!

Rapid writing

Many CMSs allow you to create a new paragraph of text just by typing it into a box on the screen. Once the typing is completed and the entry is sent, the CMS handles all the work needed for it to appear on a web page. This makes it really handy for **blogs** or for news pages of websites that need new information to be displayed frequently and quickly.

TRUE STORY

Celebs on the Web! Wordpress is popular with new website designers, but it is also used by well known companies and celebrities. Usain Bolt and Katy Perry's official websites run using Wordpress. So does the official Angry Birds computer game website and the Official Star Wars blog!

COMPUTER Hero!

Wordpress is the most popular CMS.

In 2003, Matt Mullenweg and Mike Little began developing Wordpress as an app to make it easy for people to publish blogs on the World Wide Web. It has since developed into a powerful content management system.

The World Wide Web is not yet 30 years old, but it has undergone many changes. It has increased in size dramatically, and the websites on it have become increasingly more colorful and sophisticated.

Shrinking pics

Early websites contained no pictures or maybe just a handful. They were often very small because large images slowed down the loading of the web page. With today's super-fast Internet connections, most websites feature lots of color and images, often displayed at large sizes. Some websites run background videos or **animation** at the same time.

Clive Gifford

Clive Gifford is an award-winning author of more than 60 books in both fiction and non-fiction for publishers including Hodder, Oxford University Press, Kingfisher Publications and Dorling Kindersley. He lives in Manchester, UK but travels greatly for his research and to occasionally give talks to parents, teachers and young, budding writers.

To learn more about Clive and his writing credits, please select **In Print**. For some fun and games and to learn about Clive's live visits, click on **Clive Live!**

Clive Gifford

author & journalist

Home
About
Backgrounder
Why Clive
Samples
What They Say
Journalism
Gallery
News
In Print
Football

WELCOME

Clive Gifford is a highly experienced journalist and author with over 180 books published and more than 800 features and stories written for adults and children.

Clive is an unusual author who likes to work in both fiction and non-fiction. Perhaps this reflects his unusual life which, so far, has seen him travel to over 70 countries, be held hostage in Colombia, go parachuting, coach several sports and run a computer games company.

"Welcome to the pages dealing with my work as a writer. What drives me more than anything else is the desire to communicate, entertain and inform through the written word. I hope you find these webpages of

Wide web

Early web pages look tiny when compared to those viewed on large monitors today. This is partly due to the small size of early computer screens. As screens increased in size, so did the size of web pages. When smartphone use boomed in the 2000s, website design needed to adapt. Designers made pages tall and skinny so smartphone users could easily scroll through a site.

Today, many sites are "responsive" websites. That means they can change their shape so that they can be displayed well on laptops, smartphones, tablets, and widescreen TVs.

New features

HTML itself has changed over time. Each new version released, along with the release of other apps, enables web designers to add new features to websites, from animation and games to social media updates.

STRETCH YOURSELF

Ever-Changing Websites

Websites can change greatly over time. Some may get a fresh new design, and old content may be updated, changed, or entire pages deleted.

You can view how some famous websites have changed their design over time by typing the following into your web browser:

https://tinyurl.com/gqwbty4

This takes you to an article featuring some famous, long-running websites. Move the small slider bars below each website's image to see how they were redesigned over the years.

Added Features

As new online technologies have been developed, web designers have used them to offer new features to make their websites stand out.

Adding sound

Sound can be added to web pages in different ways. The HTML tag <A HREF> adds a hyperlink that leads the browser to a sound file. If the browser is set up properly, then it should play the file.

```
<A HREF="interview.wav">Click here to listen to Jenny speak</a>
```

This is a .wav sound file.

This text appears on the page.

Audio controls

From HTML5 onward, you can add new code that allows a more advanced and useful way of adding sound. It can look like the following:

Controls display a sound player on screen (above) that allows users to play, pause, and adjust the volume of the sound file.

```
<audio controls>
<source src="happytune.mp3"
type="audio/mpeg">
Sorry, your web browser can't play this.
</audio>
```

This tag starts the audio process.

This defines the type of sound file. This is an mp3 file.

This text message is shown only if the sound file cannot be played.

Web widgets

A web **widget** is a piece of reusable code that can be added to a web page to give it an extra feature. Among the many widgets available are weather forecast panels and simple tools, including calculators that convert dollars into other currencies or measurements into metric.

JavaScript

JavaScript is a programming language used to create exciting and interactive web pages. For example, JavaScript can change the code on an HTML page to hide part of the screen, or respond and display something when a button is pressed. It is often involved in making parts of a web page move, such as a scrolling screen.

COMPUTER Hero!

Marc Andreessen was the co-author of the web browser Mosaic. This was the first widely used browser that could display images. He went on to co-found Netscape, a company that produces browsers. The company also first developed JavaScript and Ning, which is a platform for social media.

NETSCAPE®

Glossary

animation When images or models are photographed in a series of positions so they look as if they are moving when the images are shown in sequence as in a film

app A small computer program, such as a game, that can be downloaded and used on mobile devices such as tablets and smartphones

blog Short for web log, a list of diary or journal entries posted on a web page for others to read

clients Computers and other devices that "talk to" or communicate with a web server

CMS Short for content management system, this is a computer application that allows users to edit and alter parts of their website's content easily

CSS Short for Cascading Style Sheets, this is a coding language that is used to define the style and look of a web page

data Pieces of information a user puts into a computer

domain name A name unique to a specific website

FTP Short for File Transfer Protocol, this is a system that is used to transfer files from one computer to another, via a network such as the Internet

HTML Short for Hypertext Markup Language, this is a type of language that web pages are written in so that they can be displayed on different devices using the Internet

HTTP Short for Hypertext Transfer Protocol, this is a set of rules that allows computer data and files to be transferred on the World Wide Web

hyperlink A word, phrase, or image on a web page, which allows the user to jump to a new place in the website with one click

Internet A system of computer networks that connects millions of computers worldwide

JavaScript A programming language used to create interactive web pages

navigate To find your way from one place to another

pixels The dots of color that make up an image on a screen

smart Any device that has the abiltiy to connect to the Internet built into it

style sheet A text document that gives a browser information about the design of a website

tag A piece of code that gives direction to a browser in HTML

template A ready-made form or framework

upload To send a computer file from one computer to another, or if connected to a network, posting the file on the network for others to share, view, and use

URL Short for Uniform Resource Locator, this is a unique address for each file or web page held on a computer network such as the Internet

web browser A type of program used by people to view websites on the World Wide Web

web pages Documents found on the World Wide Web

web server A computer that stores and serves up (delivers) web pages to viewers connected to the Internet when they make a request

widget Reusable code or tools that can be added to a website

World Wide Web A collection of information that can be accessed by the Internet

Further Resources

Books

I'm an App Developer by Max Wainewright (Crabtree Publishing, 2018)

I'm an HTML Web Page Builder by Max Wainewright (Crabtree Publishing, 2018)

The Quick Expert's Guide to Building a Website by Chris Martin (Rosen Classroom, 2014)

Websites

www.lissaexplains.com/html.shtml
A great online tutorial about learning HTML, designed especially for kids.

http://bit.ly/2rRD8Zh
A handy article on creating your first web page, along with a lot of other tutorials on creating web pages.

www.lissaexplains.com/javascript.shtml
A fabulous series of demonstrations and tutorials for kids about using JavaScript in websites.

http://computing.artsci.wustl.edu/help/web/resize-images-web
A useful guide to different ways of resizing images for your website.

Index